Prince2 Basics

Project Management

Prince2 - 2017

Table of Contents:

Chapter 1 - Starting up a project
Chapter 2- Initiating a project
Chapter 3 - Product based planning technique
Chapter 4- Managing a stage boundary
Chapter 5- Managing product delivery
Chapter 6 - Controlling a stage
Chapter 7 - Closing a Project
About the Author

Report Templates
Issue Report
Highlight Report
Exception Report
End Stage Report
Checkpoint Report
End of Project Report

Registers
Risk Register Template
Quality Register Template
Lessons Learned Template

Chapter 1

Starting Up A Project

This occurs pre-project

PROJECT MANDATE

Appoint the Executive of the Project Board and the Project Manager
Executive will now design and appoint the remaining roles within the Project Board including who will fill the Senior User and Senior Supplier roles, and how Project Assurance
The project manager will design and appoint any other supporting roles that will be needed such as project support, configuration management and the optional Team Manager

Output from this process, the Project Brief and a plan for the Initiation Stage

The Project Brief contains the outline Business Case with sufficient information to justify carrying out the initiation stage, creating the Project Product Description which includes aspects such as the customer's quality expectations and acceptance criteria for the end product of the project & Project Approach management document
The Project Brief is a refinement of the Project Mandate, and in a similar way the Project Brief will be refined further within the initiation stage to become the Project Initiation Documentation (PID).

One important principle of PRINCE2 is that of manage by exception. The purpose of this is to set tolerance levels at the directing, managing, and delivering management levels within a project.

Tolerance is defined as limit within which a specific level may manage without the need to escalate to the next level above. There are six objectives against which tolerances may be set: time, cost, quality, scope, risk, and benefits. If any of these tolerances are forecast to be exceeded, then an Exception Plan must be raised which if approved would replace the existing plan that would have no longer completed within tolerance. Corporate or Programme management have the authority to set project level tolerances, the Project Board have authority to set stage level tolerances, and optionally, the Project Manager may set tolerances around each specific Work Package.

One of the PRINCE2 principles is learning from experience. For this reason, the Lessons Log is created and filled with any lessons that can be learned from appropriate individuals and previous similar projects.

The project manager would be expected to proactively collect such data. The Lessons Log will be updated and used throughout the project, as a source of information to create the optional Lessons Report at the end of each stage, and the Lessons Report that is created as part of the Closing a Project process.

The Daily Log is also created by the project manager and is used as a 'diary' by the project manager for the remainder of the project. But here in SU, it is also used to capture any risks and issues that need to be managed prior to the formal start of the project.

To proceed any further, the newly formed project board will need to decide whether or not it is worth investing in the creation of the PID. Specifically, how much work effort and resources are needed in the initiation stage.

The information contained within the Project Brief and the initiation Stage Plan will give the project board sufficient information to make an informed choice.

The Starting Up a Project process culminates with the project manager requesting that the project board consider authorizing the initiation stage. This uses the first activity "authorizing initiation" within the directing a project (DP) process.

The project board may decide not to proceed any further. However, let's assume that in this instance they agree based on the evidence above to invest in the initiation stage, then this will become the formal start of the project, and corporate program management will be informed that the project is initiated.

Chapter 2

Initiating a Project

The initiating a project process is used within the initiation management stage and the main deliverable here is the PID itself. The activities within this process echo the contents of the project initiation documentation. It makes sense to first determine the various approaches needed within the project be for detailed planning takes place.

The Risk Management Approach document is created, and the Risk Register is set up to capture and manage any risks throughout the project. Any risks which exist already on the Daily Log would now be transferred to the Risk Register. The Risk Management Approach defines HOW resource will be managed throughout the project.

The Quality Management Approach document is created, and the Quality Register is set up. This register will typically be empty at this point, as this will contain the planned dates of all quality management activities for the creation of the specialist products, and such dates will not be known until the second Stage Plan is created.

This second stage is always the first delivery stage, so-called because this is the first stage (and possibly also the final stage for small simple projects) where specialist products are to be created.

The word specialist products refer to the type of project, for example if the project end product is a new office building, then the specialist products would be for example, the building frame itself, roof and walls, water and electricity services to be implemented, heating and lighting products, office equipment and so on.

These should not be confused with the PRINCE2 management products such as the Project Brief, Project Initiation Documentation, reports, and so on.

So, you can see that the Quality Register will have the actual dates of the quality checking activities entered during a typical delivery stage.

It is worth mentioning that PRINCE2 2017 does not consider a specialist product as complete, until it has had an independent quality check and an appropriate authorization.

As part of the PRINCE2 2017 product-based planning technique, a product description for each specialist product is written as part of planning for a particular delivery stage. This Product Description will contain the method and the appropriate measurements required for the product to have ensure the pass its quality check.

The Change Management Approach document is created, and the Issue Register is set up. In PRINCE2, an issue can be advice of a new risk, a problem or concern, or a change. There are two types of changes: a request for change which typically comes from the customer and it is a request for a change to what was originally agreed.

The second type of change is called an off-specification; typically, this would come from the supply side and covers some aspect of the project that although agreed, cannot now be met.

Configuration management may be thought of as version control and as such is closely aligned with how change control (mentioned above) is to be implemented. Typically, configuration management will be supplied by the project support role.

The final "strategy" is the Communication Management Approach and is created last because the first three strategies will have communication needs and these can be included at this point. As you can see, all four of the strategies are HOW-TO documents.

The Project Plan can now be created in parallel with setting up the various controls there will be needed throughout the project.

Typically, these controls focus on those needed at project board level for example end stage assessment timing, and the frequency of their regular Highlight Reports, while at project manager level for example, the formality or otherwise of issuing Work Packages and the frequency of the regular Checkpoint Reports.

> Highlight Reports cover progress within the management stage, and Checkpoint Reports cover the progress of specialist product creation within a Work Package.

Chapter 3

Product Based Planning Technique

As with all plans, the Project Plan is a document, and will use the PRINCE2 product-based planning technique.

Traditional project planning would start with the brainstorming of the various activities. But one of the principles of PRINCE2 is product focus.

What this means is that the product based planning technique starts with the identification of products, initially at the highest level within a project, by creating the Project Product Description, but then going on to create a Product Breakdown Structure which is a hierarchical diagram of the products within a given project.

The next step would be to create Product Descriptions for all appropriate lower level products, including their quality criteria. The final product-based planning step is to create a Product flow Diagram, which shows the sequence of creation of the products.

In case you are confused, an activity would normally be described with a noun and verb such as 'create report', whereas a product would be described with a noun or outcome for example "specification document".

Within PRINCE2, the next steps cover traditional planning techniques, first identifying the activities needed to create each product, then estimating such activities, creating the schedule or sequence of such activities (usually shown as a network diagram or Gantt Chart view).

This continues, by going on to identify risks, their associated response activities, and finally adding the narrative of the plan document.

Because of this, new Product Descriptions along with their quality criteria will be created along with a Configuration Item Record (CIR) for each product. This record forms part of the data and the status for each product held within configuration management.

Also, at this point the Project Product Description may now needs to be further refined, for example, as better data is understood for the acceptance criteria of the project end product.

The detailed Business Case can now be developed as it will use timescale and cost information derived from the Project Plan.

This detailed Business Case will be used throughout the project in particular at the end of each management stage where it is updated and used as a basis to proceed or otherwise by the project board.

A new management product is now created based upon some information contained within the business case, and it is called the Benefits Management Approach. As the name suggests, this contains a description of each future benefit, its timing, measurement, and the resources required to carry this out.

The Benefits Management Approach is kept separate from the Project Initiation Documentation as it will be used after the project has finished to continue and track the remaining benefits until their eventual realization.

All of the above can now be assembled and forms the Project Initiation Documentation.

The project manager will now request that the project board authorize the project. They will use this named activity within the Directing a Project process (DP), and this will always be the first end stage assessment within any PRINCE2 project (as the initiation stage is always the first management stage in a PRINCE2 project).

> However, there is a parallel activity that also needs to take place if this project is to proceed any further, and that is to prepare a Stage Plan for the next stage.

Chapter 4

Managing Stage Boundary

The Managing a Stage Boundary (SB) process is used for this purpose and will use the product based planning technique. As this is the end of the initiation stage then the End Stage Report will also need to be created along with an optional Lessons Report.

Authorizing the PID will occur within the Authorize the Project activity and authorizing the next Stage Plan will occur at the Authorize a Stage or Exception Plan activity.

Both of these are activities within the Directing a Project process and will normally take place at the same meeting which is the end stage assessment.

At this end stage assessment, as is typical, the project board has the option to approve the next Stage Plan, prematurely close the project, or request that the project manager reworks some aspect of the documentation.

Assuming all is well, the Project Board will set stage tolerance for the next stage, advise the project manager of the frequency and detail to be included in the regular Highlight Reports and approve the next Stage Plan. This will now trigger the project manager to give out the first Work Package within this newly approved stage.

It is highly likely that the number and detail of Work Packages within a stage and any associated Team Plans have already been thought through during the planning of the relevant stage.

But whether they have or not, the PRINCE2 2017 method defines that the specialist team should not start work on any product creation until a Work Package containing such work has been authorized by the project manager and accepted by either the team manager or the team members themselves.

Chapter 5

Managing Product Delivery

The Team Manager role may optionally be given to an appropriate individual within the specialist team (if the specialist team is a third party, then it may well be that their project manager takes on the role of Team Manager – but remember, there can only be one Project Manager. The team manager may optionally produce a Team Plan which would show that one or many Work Packages can be delivered within the constraints laid down.

Every Work Package must contain at least one Product Description. The project manager may optionally set tolerances at the work package level.
Once the Work Package has been agreed and accepted then work can start on the creation of the specialist products contained within the Work Package.

At any given point during a stage there may be one or several Work Packages, possibly given to different teams, being worked on at the same time. Alternatively Work Packages may be given out one after another.

Probably 90% of the project budget is spent within the Managing Product Delivery (MP) process, since this is where the specialist products are created.

The **'execute a work package'** activity is where the specialist products are created, and their quality checks carried out, followed by their approval by the appropriate authority or individual..

The team manager or the team themselves will produce regular Checkpoint Reports providing information on the status and future forecast of the creation of specialist products. These are sent to the project manager and may be in the form of a report or a meeting.

Chapter 6

Controlling A Stage

The project manager will use the activity of Review Work Package Status to determine the progress or otherwise of the creation and the approval of these specialist products.
Since the Stage Plan has been approved by the Project Board, then the project manager must look at progress within the stage itself.

If the project manager determines that the stage is forecast to remain within tolerance bounds, then he or she may take some form of corrective action to minimize any such deviations within tolerance. This may entail giving out new or modified Work Packages to the specialist team.
In addition to this the project manager will need to review the stage status and use the activity of report highlights, which will generate a Highlight Report to be given to the project board so that they understand the current status and forecast future of progress within the stage.

The project manager will update the Stage Plan with actual progress and modifying future actions to ensure that the stage plan is forecast to complete within tolerance.
As each Work Package is completed, then the team manager or the specialist team themselves needs to inform the project manager that the Work Package is indeed complete.

The project manager, as part of the activity review work package status will need to agree that all the products have been completed, met their quality criteria, and have been approved by the appropriate authority.

This may trigger the authorization of a new/revised Work Package, or that the stage end is approaching, in which case the project manager would use the Managing a Stage Boundary (SB) process to prepare for an end stage assessment. If at any time during the stage, either issues or risks should arise, then the project manager should use the activity of capture and examine issues and risks to carry out an impact analysis of these on both the stage and project. The appropriate Issue or Risk Register should be updated with such information.

If the project manager determines that some corrective action can be taken via the issue of new or modified Work Packages to resolve the situation then such actions would need to be taken.

If after impact analysis and the review of this within the status of the stage or the project would show that forecast of tolerances would be exceeded, then the project manager must create an Exception Report and bring this to the attention of the project board.

If a Work Package is forecast to exceed tolerance levels, the Team Manager would raise this as an issue to bring it to the attention of the project manager.
Using the activity escalate issues and risks, the project manager would bring this Exception Report to the attention of the project board.

Put simply this Exception Report should contain information on the reasons for this forecast of exceeding tolerances, the impact in terms of the appropriate tolerance, and a set of options, which if implemented would return the stage of project within tolerance bounds, and a recommendation of which option should be chosen, and why it is the best option.

This is sent to the project board who now need to decide on what to do next. One option they have is to prematurely close the project, in which case the project manager would use the Closing a Project (CP) process to carry this out.
For the moment we shall assume that they prefer another option, either recommended by the project manager, or one which they have determined. This would trigger the project manager to use the Managing a Stage Boundary (SB) process The project board would request the preparation of an Exception Plan using the Managing a Stage Boundary process. At this point it would be helpful to state that the Managing a Stage Boundary process has only TWO uses.

The first is to prepare for an end stage assessment (ESA) by creating the next Stage Plan.
The second is to prepare for an exception assessment (EXA). In the former the objective is to approve or otherwise, the next Stage Plan, and in the latter it is to approve or otherwise the Exception Plan.

Whichever of the above, this process would follow the following steps and activities:

1-   Create either a next Stage Plan or an Exception Plan

2-   Update the Project Plan to show actual progress and if necessary, a modified future forecast

3-   As part of updating the Project Plan and the next Stage Plan/Exception Plan, it may be necessary to update some aspects of the PID (possibly in terms of the strategies, the plan, and the controls, or the Business Case and related Benefits Management Approach

4-   As a result of the above, new or modified Product Descriptions will need to be created, new or modified risks and issues entered on to the appropriate registers including any lessons that have been learned during the stage

5-   The Benefits Management Approach needs to be updated to reflect any products that may have already being released into the operational (business as usual – BAU) areas

6-   The project manager will produce an End Stage Report and if appropriate create a Lessons Report

All of the above will be brought before the project board at either an end stage assessment or an exception assessment. The project board will need to decide to either approve the next Stage Plan, or approve the Exception Plan, or request more information, or to order a premature close of the project. For each delivery stage these four processes will continue in the same manner as described above.

The Managing a Stage Boundary process will be used either to prepare a next Stage Plan or an Exception Plan and is brought before the project board using the Directing a Project process to either approve or otherwise the next Stage Plan or an Exception Plan.

Once this has been authorized, the project manager will give out the work contained within that Stage Plan and the specialist team will create the specialist products via each Work Package.

When the last Work Package has been completed (each specialist product has been approved), then this will trigger the project manager to acknowledge that the project end is approaching.

A very important point needs to be made here. If the project, within any management stage, needs to be brought to a premature close, then the closing a project process (CP) is used.

Let us suppose that a given project has three delivery stages after the initiation stage. In the final delivery stage, work packages containing information on the specialist products to be created will be issued and managed as described above.

Chapter 7

Closing A Project

However, once the final specialist product within the final work package has been approved, then the project manager will trigger the closing a project (CP) processes to shut the project down in a controlled manner.

A final management stage is not used to merely to use the Closing a Project process. In summary, the final stage of a project will use the Controlling a Stage, Managing Product Delivery, and Closing a Project processes.

Assuming a natural close to the project, then the "prepare planned closure" activity will be used.

The project manager would request a product status account to ensure that all products within the project would have been approved and that the project acceptance criteria have been met. The Project Plan should be updated with the 'actuals' of this final stage.

The projects products must now be handed over to the operational and maintenance environment, where they will be used to ultimately realize the benefits contained as stated within the Business Case.

The project manager would updates relevant configuration item records to show that such products have the status of 'operational', any acceptance records should be created or obtained, and the Benefits Management Approach updated to reflect any products that have already realized benefits and to include any post project activities for such benefits that have yet to be realized.

The re-evaluate the project activity will create the end of project report to capture actual progress and aspects such as project performance metrics and will include the Lessons Report based upon the information contained within the Lessons Log.

In the case of premature close, then the reasons for this should be entered and updated on the Issue Register, and if necessary any additional work may be needed to complete unfinished products or to make them safe.

Once the project manager has determined that the project should and can be closed, then a recommendation of such should be raised to the project board in the form of a closure recommendation.

The final activity in any project, is the authorized project closure within the Directing a Project process.

The project board would need to review original and updated versions of the PID, review and approve the End Project Report, confirm any follow-on actions or loose ends, verify that the projects products have been handed over in an appropriate manner, ensure that the Business Case remains viable, advise that the project can now be closed, and advise those supplier resources that these can now be withdrawn.

Okay, so now you can see how the processes work with each other. You can see that the Starting Up a Project, Initiating a Project, and Closing a Project are usually used once per project.

You will have noted that at the completion of the Starting Up a Project process, the Directing a Project Process is continually used until the final close of the project.

It will not have escaped your attention that the Managing a Stage Boundary process is EITHER used at the end of a management stage to prepare for an End Stage Assessment (ESA), OR it is used if needed when Tolerance is forecast to be exceeded AND Corporate/Programme Management or the Project Board request an Exception Plan – in which case the SB process is used to create an Exception Report and prepare for an Exception Assessment (EXA).

The controlling a Stage & Managing Product Delivery processes are used continually during an individual management stage.

Report Templates

ISSUE REPORT

Document Information

Project name:	The name of your project
Issue date:	When the report was issued
Author:	Normally, the name and title of the Project Manager
Document code:	Configuration item record number for this document
Version:	Version of the document (e.g. v2.12)

Approval of the Decision

Date	Name and Signature

Notes

Any extra information or concerns, or even an executive summary can go here. Leave empty if not needed.

The Issue

ID:	The identifier that is used in the Issue Log
Issue type:	Request for change, off-specification, or problem/concern
Date Raised:	
Last updated:	
Decision date:	
Closure date:	
Raised by:	Name and title of the person
Priority:	
Severity:	

Impact

Explain the impact of the issue.

Recommendation

Identify different responses to the issue, and recommend the one that you find best as the project manager.

Decision

The final decision by the Project Board

HIGHLIGHT REPORT

Document Information

Project name:	The name of your project
Period:	The period of reporting
Issue date:	When the report was issued
Author:	Normally, the name and title of the Project Manager
Document code:	Configuration item record number for this document
Version:	Version of the document (e.g. v2.12)

Notes

Any extra information or concerns, or even an executive summary can go here. Leave empty if not needed.

Products

Product/Work Package	Status in this period	Expected Status for the next period
Name of the product or Work Package that was planned for this stage	Status of the product until the end of the period, including the quality activities related to that product and corrective actions taken.	Expected status, including the quality status.

Issues and risks

Key Issue or risk
Latest update on issues (including change requests) and risks related to the Work Package

Project Objectives

	Target	Tolerance	Current State	Forecast
Scope				
Time				
Cost				
Quality				
Risks				
Benefits				

Stage Objectives

	Target	Tolerance	Current State	Forecast
Scope				
Time				
Cost				
Quality				
Risks				
Benefits				

Lessons Learned

Lesson Learned
Describe one lesson per row.

EXCEPTION REPORT

Document Information

Project name:	The name of your project
Issue date:	When the report was issued
Author:	Normally, the name and title of the Project Manager
Approver:	Normally, the Executive
Document code:	Configuration item record number for this document
Version:	Version of the document (e.g. v2.12)

Approval

Date	Name and Signature

Notes

Any extra information or concerns, or even an executive summary can go here. Leave empty if not needed.

Cause of the Exception

If the Exception was mainly caused by one issue, explain that issue. Otherwise, explain how the cumulative effect of multiple issues has caused it, and what the underlying reason was that those issues stacked up.

Consequences

Explain the consequences of the deviation on the project and the business.

Options

Explain the possible options that you can think of, and mention which one is your recommended option.

Project Objectives

	Target	Tolerance	Current State	Forecast
Scope				
Time				
Cost				
Quality				
Risks				
Benefits				

Stage Objectives

	Target	Tolerance	Actual State
Scope			
Time			
Cost			
Quality			
Risks			
Benefits			

Lessons Learned

Lesson Learned
Describe one lesson per row.

END STAGE REPORT

Document Information

Project name:	The name of your project
Period:	The period of reporting
Issue date:	When the report was issued
Author:	Normally, the name and title of the Project Manager
Approver:	Normally, the Project Board members
Document code:	Configuration item record number for this document
Version:	Version of the document (e.g. v2.12)

Approval

Date	Name and Signature

Notes

Any extra information or concerns, or even an executive summary can go here. Leave empty if not needed.

Justification of the project

Provide a short analysis of the current justification of the project based on the Business Case.

Products

Product	Status
Name of the active product	Status of the product until the end of the period, including the quality and approval status of the product, possible off-specifications, and handovers.

Project Objectives

	Target	Tolerance	Current State	Forecast
Scope				
Time				
Cost				
Quality				
Risks				
Benefits				

CHECKPOINT REPORT

Document Information

Project name:	The name of your project
Period:	The period of reporting
Issue date:	When the report was issued
Author:	Normally, the name and title of the Team Leader
Approver:	Normally, the name and title of the Project Manager
Document code:	Configuration item record number for this document
Version:	Version of the document (e.g. v2.12)

Approval

Date	Name and Signature

Notes

Any extra information or concerns, or even an executive summary can go here. Leave empty if not needed

Follow-ups from the previous period

Were there any action items or unresolved issued from the last reporting period?

Products

Product	Current Status	Expected Status for the next period
Name of the products in the Work Package	Status of the product until the end of the period, including the quality activities related to that product.	Expected status, including quality status

Work Package Objectives

	Target	Tolerance	Current State	Forecast
Scope				
Time				
Cost				
Quality				
Risks				

Issues and risks

Issue or risk

Latest update on issues and risks related to the Work Package

Lessons Learned

Lesson Learned

Describe one lesson per row.

END OF PROJECT REPORT

Document Information

Project name:	The name of your project
Issue date:	When the report was issued
Author:	Normally, the name and title of the Project Manager
Approver:	Normally, the Project Board members
Document code:	Configuration item record number for this document
Version:	Version of the document (e.g. v2.12)

Approval

Date	Name and Signature

Notes

Any extra information or concerns, or even an executive summary can go here. Leave empty if not needed.

Justification of the project

Provide a short analysis of the current justification of the project based on the Business Case.

Project Objectives

	Target	Tolerance	Actual
Scope			
Time			
Cost			
Quality			
Risks			
Benefits			

Products

Product	Status
Name of the product	Quality records, approval records, explanation about off-specifications, and possible handovers.

Team Performance

A short description of the team performance.

Follow-on Action Recommendations

Unfinished work or open issue/risk	Owner
Item	Suggested owner, if any

Lessons Learned

Lesson Learned
Describe one lesson per row.

Registers

RISK REGISTER TEMPLATE

Project Name:
Project No.

DATE	RISK DESCRIPTION	RISK CATEGORY	RISK TYPE	RISK OWNER	RISK RESPONSE
20/03/21	What is the risk?	Budget Cost	LOW	Name of team member	How is it resolved
		Schedule	MODERATE		Avoid
		Quality	HIGH		Mitigate
		Resources			Transfer
		Human Resource			Accept
		Governance			
		Supplier			
		Procurement			
		Financial			
		Health & Safety			
		Organization Environment			

QUALITY REGISTER TEMPLATE

Project Name:
Project No.

DATE	QUALITY ISSUE DESCRIPTION	PROPOSED CORRECTIVE ACTION	COST IMPACT	SCHEDULE IMPACT	APPROVAL STATUS
20/03/21	What is the quality issue, explain reasons	Proposed resolution to the problem	Cost of Corrective Action	Time of Delay to the Baseline	Approved By & Date of approval

LESSONS LEARNED

DATE	TYPE	ROOT CAUSE	LESSON DESCRIPTION
20/03/21	Design	Reason why issue took place	Describe the details of the lesson learned
	Assumption		
	Change Control		
	Change Management		
	Corrective Action		
	Decision Making		
	Estimates		
	Knowledge Management		
	Integration Management		
	Performance Management		
	Project Management		
	Project Constraints		
	Project Management Tools		
	Project Expectations		
	Project Governance		
	Project Sponsor		
	Project Methodology		
	Quality		
	Project Planning		
	Roles & Responsibilities		
	Vendor Performance		
	Project Funding		

About The Author

Lamya Sabah is an architect with over 20 years of experience in architectural design, coordination, shop drawings production and structural detailing. Holds a Master of Architecture degree from The University of Auckland, in New Zealand

She has worked on large projects with professional architectural consultants, project management firms and contractors in several international cities.

Printed in Great Britain
by Amazon